IMAGES OF ENGLAND

SKIPTON
AND THE DALES

IMAGES OF ENGLAND

SKIPTON
AND THE DALES

KEN ELLWOOD

TEMPUS

I have written extensively about the aircrews of the war, but we must not forget that men and women from this beautiful area also served in both the army and the navy, some never to return.

Ken Ellwood

Frontispiece: In 1941 Skipton held a Wings for Victory week to raise funds to purchase five Halifax Bombers and twelve fighters for a total of £250,000. A huge 'totaliser' was erected in front of Skipton Town Hall and crowds would gather whenever the arrow moved up to its new total. Peter Horner, then a ten-year-old schoolboy from Embsay, was the lucky lad chosen to be chairman on 'Children's Day', while schoolgirl Jean Abbotson was chosen to move the arrow on the totaliser. Pictured left to right on the platform are Mr Champion, the town hall commissionaire and caretaker, Councillor David Jones, chairman of Skipton council, Jean Abbotson, Peter Horner and RAF officer Stephen E. Brown, who later became Craven coroner. The event proved worthwhile in more ways than one for young master Horner, as afterwards Councillor Jones asked him to become errand boy for his grocery business!

First published 2003

Tempus Publishing Limited
The Mill, Brimscombe Port,
Stroud, Gloucestershire, GL5 2QG

© Ken Ellwood, 2003

British Library Cataloguing in Publication Data.
A catalogue record for this book is available from the British Library.

ISBN 0 7524 3058 0

Typesetting and origination by Tempus Publishing Limited
Printed in Great Britain by Midway Colour Print, Wiltshire

Contents

A painting of some cottages which once stood near the aqueduct arch by Bolton Priory. They have since been demolished.

In my first volume of archive photographs of Skipton, I used a photograph of my 1941 Tiger Moth to head the introduction. This time it is the 1922 Burrell traction engine, which I owned for over twenty years and often showed at the hospital gala. The family and Jim Turnbull are cleaning the engine.

Introduction

This is my fourth book about Skipton in old photographs and there seems to be a thirst for more. My third book set out to show all the approaches to this lovely town, noting interesting places and things to be seen on the way. One of my friends, who praised the book, suggested that I should show the way out as well! This remark, regarded as a joke, set a seed in my mind, which has now grown into an idea to include some of our beautiful Dales villages. This I have done and the reader will see these places as they were since the advent of photography.

I have always been amazed at the extensive use that was made of the camera in the countryside in times when there was little or no transport to outlying places. To make space for these photographs, I have concentrated on the centre of Skipton only, and have used material not used before in my other books.

The last chapter of my third book recorded Skipton aircrews who lost their lives in the Second World War. I have now included the airmen who volunteered from the villages, most leaving home for the first time in their lives, never to return.

So let us take a walk from Swadford Street and explore the High Street round to Water Street, then along Coach Street and back to Swadford Street.

Ken Ellwood

Acknowledgements

Most of the photographs were copied and improved by Frank Knowles and Maple Leaf Images. My daughter Deborah and daughter-in-law Mandy have both spent hours typing the captions. Many people mentioned in my other three books on old Skipton have lent photographs. Val Rowley keeps on discovering new material, especially after her lectures and slide shows. Mr and Mrs Hall of Conistone know a lot about the Dales, and Alan Stockdale of Burnsall has a fine collection and much knowledge of that village. Mrs Cynthia Rymer of Hetton is always most helpful. Donald Binns has supreme knowledge of our local railways and his books are well worth collecting. Stan Greaves DFM of Leeds and I had many enjoyable flights to take some of the aerial photographs. I have also used aircraft of Comed Aviation of Blackpool, ably flown by Robert Murgatroyd, who at one time lived in Gargrave. Harold Allison, former head keeper at Bolton Abbey, was also very helpful with his knowledge of wildlife, especially grouse. Michael Walmsley has shared his photographs and knowledge of Bradley.

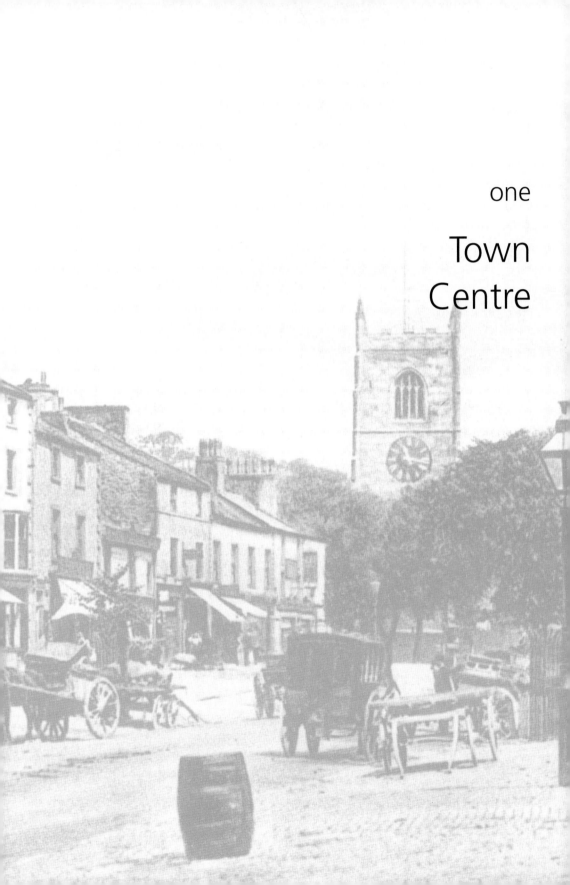

one

Town
Centre

From Swadford Street we look into Caroline Square, at the corner end of High Street. The photograph was taken on Fair Day in around 1895, when farmers traded cattle in the High Street, and often spilled out into Swadford Street and Keighley Road. George Mattock advertises cattle food and Spratt's dog biscuits. On the right of the picture is the London Midland Bank.

Before proceeding further, study this aerial photograph of Skipton taken in June 1994. It shows most of the areas of Skipton that we are going to visit in this book. The extension to the Skipton Building Society has not yet been built, but otherwise the town is much the same. The open-air market is not there, so we get a better view of the High Street and Sheep Street, which is split from the former by Middle Row. Notice how the church and the castle stand so well at the top of town. An enlargement of this picture shows the time on the church clock as 11.45 a.m.

Above: An early 1900s view from Caroline Square, looking up Sheep Street on the left and High Street. Midland Bank (now HSBC) is on the right and was built in 1888. Brick Hall Hotel on the left (now Woolly Sheep) advertises BYB (Bentley's Yorkshire Breweries).

Below: Barclays Bank and my dental surgery were cleaned about 1975. Timothy White's, managed by Bobby Horner, was a popular chemist's shop.

Above: Sheep Street is split off from the High Street by the buildings on the right called Middle Row. Sheep Street Hill is further along, a popular place for itinerant preachers. Ramsbottom's electrical and radio shop was managed by Mr Blood; I purchased a Cossor radio here in 1955. This picture is from around 1950.

Below: This photograph was taken in the Brick Hall Hotel yard (now Woolly Sheep). This bullock was killed and roasted in Skipton to celebrate Queen Victoria's Golden Jubilee on 21 June 1887.

Above: The Tea Shop in Sheep Street, *c.* 1930, a popular meeting place for many people in Skipton, situated in the Old Town Hall.

Below: These metal covers can still be seen in Sheep Street today. GCo. means Gas Company; the covers protected fittings which would take a gas light post for stall holders.

Above: A very early etching of Skipton High Street, also known as Market Place. It shows the Market Cross, and behind it four old cottages. The four foundation stones of the Cross can still be seen outside Barclays Bank.

Opposite above: This photograph must have been taken after 1888, as the trees are present and the new Midland Bank building next to the Wheatsheaf Inn has been built. Notice the walkway for pedestrians across the unmade High Street, and also the cobbles. Two delivery vans, one with sliding shelves, must remind some people of their youth. William Mattock has also moved premises – see page 10.

Opposite below: There are many views of this famous market scene and no book about Skipton is complete without one. They all vary but I have not seen this one before, taken about 1900. This fortnightly cattle fair was eventually moved in 1906 to Jerry Croft, now the car park behind the Town Hall. Dr Rowley said that there were thirty years of argument about it. Within two years of the market moving out of the streets three of the High Street inns had closed – the Thanet's Arms, the Fountain and the Wheatsheaf.

Above: A quiet scene in Skipton before 1888 as there is no Midland Bank and no trees. W. Scott the tub maker's shop is on the left just past the steps. Footpath crossings can also be seen over the unmade road, which was a mess during cattle fairs.

Below: There is quite a change in the buildings here in this 1930s picture, compared to the last few photographs. The Exchange buildings are on the left. A.J. Clayton has taken over from Mattock's, and over on the right is the Midland Bank (now HSBC) and High Street House. This lower part of the High Street was used as a bus station. The nearest bus was for Bradley.

Above: A more recent view, probably 1960s or '70s. Notable premises include the Hole in the Wall, S & B Fruits, Skipton Building Society, Midland Bank, Armitage, the Ribble bus office, and the High Street House. Name all the makes of cars! A Mini stands next to a Ford Anglia with sloping rear windows.

Below: A pleasant picture beyond Otley Street showing a footpath across the street, with a clear view from before the library was built. Note the elegant gas lamps. This was around 1890.

This 1920s picture must be included, if only to show the elegant gas lamp, the Craven Herald Printing Works and the new library. The trees are now well established. I wonder what the stallholder is selling? In another picture a similar stall advertises ice cream. In 2003, the Craven Herald Printing Works celebrate their 150th anniversary.

This photograph was taken about 1900. The trees, planted in 1897, are still small, and the library, opened in 1910, has not yet been built. There is plenty of horse and cart interest.

A later scene, probably from the 1920s, showing two interesting cars, including a three-wheeler. Skipton library can be seen; this was opened by Sir Mathew Wilson on 16 February 1910. On the right is the Old George, now part of Rackhams. In the late 1950s I had lunch here, with excellent waitress service. The time is five minutes past two and the photographer is standing at the corner of Otley Street.

The sign of Mrs Ambler Ltd, 37 High Street, can be seen on the right. Mrs Ambler started the business in 1893, selling high-class millinery, gowns, coats, hosiery and underwear. In 1961 the shop was taken over by Brown Muffs of Bradford, and they extended the premises to the rear. In 1970 they took over the Old George, demolishing the rear but keeping the existing High Street façade. The shop is now Rackhams. Next door is the ironmonger's, T.W. Hager, who sells hay-cutting machinery.

Another view of the popular Tea Shop with J. Wood & Sons' music shop next door, late 1920s or 1930s. Note the signs above advertising a Travellers' Lodge. There were many such Friendly Societies in those days. The float in Skipton Gala depicts a Gretna Green 'marriage'.

MAKERS OF
CHAIN PUMPS,
CHAFF CUTTERS,
LAND ROLLERS,
AND OTHER
AGRICULTURAL
IMPLEMENTS.
—
IRON AND
STEEL
MERCHANTS,
ETC.

FRED MANBY & BRO., SKIPTON.

Fred Manby & Bro., established in 1817, is seen here at the top end of Middle Row. They could supply anything. In about 1970 I purchased two First World War propellers from them – unused! The rotary engine was scrapped during the last war and would have been worth a great deal of money now.

Above and below: Fred Manby & Bro. had an iron foundry in Union Street next to the canal, seen here with Christ Church in the background. It was in these premises that they also had a car and motorcycle repair shop.

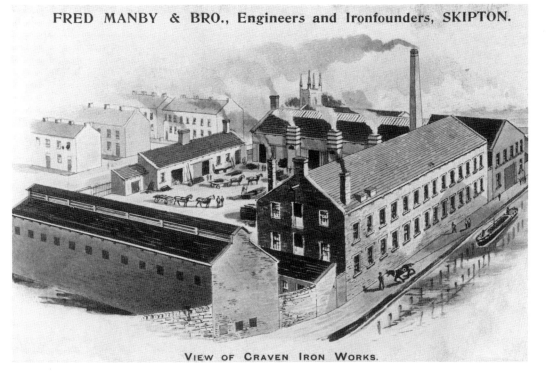

FRED MANBY & BRO., Engineers and Ironfounders, SKIPTON.

VIEW OF CRAVEN IRON WORKS.

On a Skipton Fair day in around 1895 there can be seen a preacher standing on one of the farm carts outside the farm implement shop. Note the large water butt on wheels, and also the machine operated by a large wheel and handle, possibly used for chopping root crops.

Here are the buildings that were once T.W. Hagar agricultural merchants and Mrs Ambler Ltd. Snowden's shop is on the left, where we purchased our Silver Cross pram – we still have it, four children and eight grandchildren later! This used to be the Thanet's Arms. The Carla Beck was a milk bar and popular meeting place for cyclists. This was around the 1950s.

Ambler, Robert Hurst & Co. and the Old George have now been swallowed up by Rackhams. A mowing machine shows the agricultural merchants are still there. On the other side of the tree stands George Metcalfe's High Class Ices. The decorations are up to celebrate the coronation of King George V in 1911.

A clear view of the top of the High Street in the late 1940s, also showing a variety of cars, a tractor and a motorcycle.

I include this picture to show the cast-iron canopy at the entrance to the Town Hall, which was removed in the early 1950s. The cottages shown here were demolished to make way for the much-criticised Health Centre.

One early motor car is still outnumbered by horse-drawn vehicles. There is also a good view of the footpath crossing the road from the church to the pavement near the Black Horse. Seats for the old folks surround the statue of Sir Mathew Wilson, which was later moved to a position in front of the library in order to make way for the Cenotaph.

Left: On 18 June 1983, our daughter Deborah, a dental surgeon, married Dr Christopher Oates of Whitley Bay at Holy Trinity church. Here in attendance is a Burrell traction engine, named after her. Alwyn Rogers is the driver, and his brother–in–law, Mark Anderson, the steersman. They presented Deborah with a piece of coal – suitably varnished! Deborah was driven to church in a 1932 Rolls Royce and the bridesmaids arrived in a 1955 Riley. The Skipton Band played in the churchyard and there was also a peal of church bells – a good time was had by all!

Below: An aerial photograph taken in 1949 shows how well the church and castle stand at the top of High Street. Mill Bridge and Springs Canal show how near the visitor is to an interesting walk along the towpath behind the castle.

This statue of Skipton's first MP, Sir Mathew Wilson, Bart., of Eshton Hall, was unveiled by the Marquis of Ripon in 1888. It was unusual for a statue to be erected to anyone in his own lifetime, as happened in this case. The house seen in the background (now David Goldie) was the home and surgery of Dr Forsyth Wilson, and the birthplace in 1882 of his son Charles Macmoran Wilson, who was to become Lord Moran, Sir Winston Churchill's personal physician.

A very early and clear picture with a lot of interest. A beautiful gas lamp is suspended from the church gate, but there is no cast-iron porch for the Town Hall. Sir Mathew Wilson's statue is in its original position. There is no library yet, but there ia a clear sign advertising Excelsior Hair Cutting and Shaving Salon. The tombs are also present in the churchyard. J.L. Kidd had the Black Horse Hotel.

Here is Sir Mathew Wilson, and the seats are occupied by the older members of the community. The picture is by Smith, a very prolific photographer. The banner on the wall behind shows that the men are gathered for a Coronation celebration – probably that of George V in 1911.

The Cattle Fair even extended right up to the church and surrounded Sir Mathew Wilson. Dobson's the chemist was situated in the building where Clare Whitaker's shop and café is now. In a way, they were the forerunners of Laycock's Agricultural Chemists. This shop is now a Thresher wine shop.

Some members of the Congregational church are in this parade of the Skipton Brotherhood. Louis Gaunt the Parson is on the left, and other names are John Pickford, Bill Pritchard, and Algernon Dewhirst behind the man in the light coloured suit.

A group of men outside the Thanet's Arms. When we came to Skipton in 1953 it was Snowden's toy shop, and it is now a toy shop once more. The last landlord was Mr H.F. Miller, and the last drinks at the Thanet's Arms were served on 23 December 1908. Perhaps this photograph was taken before a charabanc trip – the driver is on the right in his long coat.

A nice group of ladies and three gentlemen ready for an outing in the smallest charabanc I have ever seen. The board behind is for Skipton Urban District Council.

Round the corner from the High Street is Mill Bridge, and this was the scene there on 22 June 1911, during a Coronation Day procession for King George V. Boy Scouts are followed by some dignitaries using umbrellas, and then horse-drawn traps and phaetons.

Left: Margaret Alderson reared a fox cub, which lived happily with the dog and family cat.

Below: Outside the New Ship (now David Hill's office) when Fred Alderson was the incumbent. The occasion is a fox shoot organised by Tom Clark, the castle gamekeeper. From left to right: Fred Alderson, -?-, t'owd Horse Doctor, Tom Clark, John Preston (of the Fire Service), -?-.

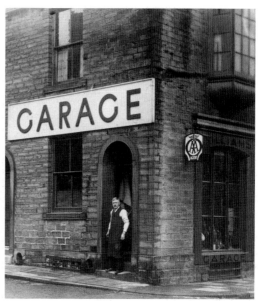

Above left: This is Jack Ward, the blacksmith, making a horseshoe. The smithy was where the Wright wine shop is now, at the bottom of Raikes Road. Jack took over the business from his uncle, A. Ellwood (no relation). I took this picture on my way to work in about 1972 and had a similar picture published in *This England*, a quarterly magazine. *Above right:* This garage is at the corner of Water Street and Victoria Terrace. Williams were coach builders, but moved on with the times. Large brass nuts were used to secure the coach wheels. The builders usually had their names on these and they are collectors' items today.

Left: These cottages stood on land next to Mill Bridge between the canal and the river. They were demolished in 1956 and the land made into a garden area with seats.

Above: Ermysted's Grammar school is situated along Gargrave Road; this picture was taken on 28 June 1994, and is a good view of the 'top'. Work is under way on the Fisher Medical Centre, lower right. The Golf Club is at the top right.

Opposite below: Along Water Street we turn left to cross the bridge to Coach Street. All the houses of nearby Commercial Street were demolished, but here is a rare picture of the Nutter family, who lived in Upper Commercial Street in 1912. From left to right, back row: Hilda, Dick, Fred and Sarah; front row: John, Mr Jim Nutter, Tom and Mrs Nutter.

Above: We joined in most of the Skipton Hospital Galas in the 1970s. Here we head up Gargrave Road with Burrell 3918 *Deborah*, steered by Deborah. Two small passengers are looked after by Alwyn Rogers in the coal tender. Alwyn is now the engineer in charge of the beautiful mill engine at Queen's Mill, Burnley. This preserved textile mill is well worth a visit.

A tranquil view of the canal and Coach Street Bridge in the early 1900s. The Royal Shepherd is along Canal Street near the elegant gas lamp. The low building has been demolished and a piece has been added on to the tall building on the right, which is now occupied by 'Lotus Petals'.

A view from Dewhirsts, showing Coach Street and Swadford Street. Union Square is in the lower part (now redeveloped) and buildings in the High Street such as Midland Bank (built 1888) can be seen. The spire of the Baptist chapel at lower right is also clear. This chapel was destroyed by fire in 1920. This is a rare picture from Bryan Robinson and friends.

Swadford Street looks busy and was captured by the camera in around 1910. Behind the café sign is one for a Gents' Outfitters. This is a good picture for studying dress of the period.

Another early picture of Swadford Street before the trees were planted in 1897. The sign reads 'Chadwick & Co. employ over 1000 Tailors, Cutters and Workpeople'. Behind is Porri's on the corner, who sold china and kitchenware.

Above: Many alterations have taken place since this aerial photograph was taken in 1928. Commercial Street at the top left is seen in its entirety. Union Square and Belmont Bridge area are much altered. New houses have been built and the corn mill has been converted to flats. Dewhirst's buildings are on the lower left. The gasometers have been demolished. Many properties in the Albert Street area are no longer there and Ship Corner is much altered. Hargreaves' dental surgery, a Georgian house, is still there, soon to be replaced by Burton's Buildings. The small cottages at Mill Bridge can be seen but were demolished in 1956.

Right: This was the scene at the end of Swadford Street and Keighley Road during the flood in 1979. Laycock's van sailed from their premises behind Woolworths, across Keighley Road and almost into Meakins Shoeshop.

two

Bradley, Cononley and
Carleton-in-Craven

Above: Just two miles along the Keighley Road and on the north side of the Aire Gap lies the village of Bradley. We lived there from 1953 to 1960 and found it to be full of friendly, hard working people. Brown's mill and Green's mill were working full time in textiles. The former is now demolished and Green's is closed. The tandem compound steam engine is to be preserved, and soon it will be at Bancroft, Barnoldswick, to join the cross compound engine, which is run during select weekends. This view dates from before 1914, the year the school was built.

Below: The way in to Bradley over the hill from Snaygill. The small Anglican church on the right, built in around 1914, was made of wood and corrugated iron on a good stone foundation. When it was demolished in 1963 or thereabouts, I acquired some of the stone to build some steps in my garden.

Above: Bradley on 19 June 1959, in a photograph taken from Tiger Moth G–APCU. Bales of hay are in Mr Maude's field at lower left next to Derek Watkinson's bungalow. The two working mills are in the centre of the village. A lot of houses have been built since 1959. The Leeds and Liverpool canal and bridge are lower right.

Below: Four roads lead into Bradley. One comes from Snaygill and over the stone canal bridge, which was the route taken when two traction engines winched this new boiler over the hill and down to Brown's Mill (Rose Shed) where it was installed. Another way in to Bradley further along Keighley Road was over a wooden canal swing bridge with a weight limit. On the left is Herbert Holmes, whose father owned the mill. Cuthbert Walmsley is on the left on top of the boiler. Joe Brown has the spade and the young boy is William Brayshay.

Above: A view of Brown's Mill, *c.* 1904. It was also known as Rose Shed because it was built in thirteen weeks – it 'rose' quickly!

Right: Before Brown's Mill closed for good in August 1994, Michael Walmsley asked me to make a photographic record. Here is Jennifer Sadler working at one of her looms.

Opposite above: Another view of the old part of Bradley, the Main Street, Slater's Arms, Green's Mill and Brown's Mill (Rose Shed). The canal is top left along with the all important cricket field.

Opposite below: Main Street with the nail maker's shop on the left and Ivy House Farm on the right. The cart belonged to Smith Green, a greengrocer from Crosshills.

Above: A well-dressed group enjoying the Whit walk, a religious festival for Methodists. West View was the home to Mr Bray, the headmaster of the school, who is on the float with Lizzie Fryers. Leornard Hudson is holding the horse.

Right: First World War troops led by Boy Scouts, perhaps on a recruiting campaign.

Opposite above: Another Whit Walk scene near Main Street. I think the band is from Silsden or Kildwick.

Members of Sweet William Lodge (Ancient Order of Foresters) meet outside the Slater's Arms. On the right of the back row is Frank Mattock, and on the middle row, fifth from the right, is Ellis Stirk, the village blacksmith. This was around 1900.

Above: Sam Throup of High Bradley converted an old Ford Model T lorry to pull a mowing machine. He was a most remarkable man who worked as a weaver at Brown's Mill in his youth and also on his father's farm. He took over Far Fold Farm and 'ran' milk to Cononley station to supply Leeds for many years before the Second World War. Cononley station was across the valley from Bradley and where Sam Throup delivered his milk kits – he called it 'Cunla'.

Opposite below: This is the wooden bridge over the Leeds and Liverpool Canal, which was also used around 1900 for sheep washing. Green's Mill is behind. Sam Throup's father can be seen on the bridge with the dog.

Left: Sam Throup talked about 'Old Job Senior the Ilkla Hermit', seen here as a sketch by T. Bottomley of Crosshills in 1849. I think he was an itinerant farm worker who lived as a hermit on Rombalds Moor later in life.

Below: A scene at Chester's Ghyll Farm. Joe Chester is on the right, in the middle is William Lord Chester and on the left a hired man (Fred Holdsworth?).

A tranquil scene on the Leeds and Liverpool canal between Bradley and Kildwick. The horse towing the barge is on the left of the picture.

A passenger train approaching Cononley station early in the 1920s, hauled by an LMS locomotive.

Above: A postcard view of Cononley station crossing gate, with an attractive small locomotive standing there. Horace Green's Electric Motor works is alongside and in the distance are Thomas Stells Aireside Mills.

Left: Approaching Kildwick level crossing gates I noticed the signalman taking a photograph so I called to see him later and he made this copy for me. We were on our way home from a rally at Pudsey organised by Leeds and District Traction Engine Club. Jim Turnbull of High Bradley is driving.

Across the Aire valley lies Carleton-in-Craven, which is nearer to Skipton than Cononley. Here is the football team in 1909 taken by Smith, the well-known Skipton photographer.

J.K. Ellwood joins in Carleton Gala with his Burrell engine No. 3918, steered by Charlie White of Earby. This was about 1970 and the parade was led by Skipton Brass Band. Joe Coates was one of the organisers and he took us up and down a steep hill – he said he was testing us!

three

Gargrave, Bell Busk, Coniston and Malham

An excellent way to explore the route west of Skipton would be on the old Thames-Clyde Express. Here we could travel behind the *Jubilee Kolapur*, seen here eaving Skipton station.

Blue Peter was fully restored and made many tours, including a stop in Skipton in 1992.

Here is another preserved locomotive, the *Duke of Gloucester* leaving Skipton on a tour to Carlisle in the late 1980s.

On page 56 of my last book about Skipton I showed the new Aireville swimming pool under construction in 1963. On 7 March 2003 I took this aerial photograph of the new pool under construction standing next to the old pool, which was closed on the following Saturday and has now been demolished.

Along the Gargrave road and half a mile past the Thorlby road end, there is a curve in the road round Woolmer Hill. When the field on the right (on the left in this picture) was cultivated, various artefacts were dug out and it was revealed that this area had been a medieval farm, shown clearly in this aerial photograph. Basil Spensley, a farmer of Thorlby, alerted me to this.

Travelling to Gargrave by pony and trap, you might have been lucky enough to see this camel and elephant pulling a travelling circus van through Gargrave about five miles west of Skipton. Bostock and Wombwell later used traction engines.

An aerial view of Gargrave in 1966. Johnson & Johnson still had their chimney, the railway is at the top right, and the main road to Settle and Kendal passes through the village alongside the River Aire. The canal passes the onetime home of the Coulthurst family, now a nursing home.

A country show is held every year at Broughton Hall; it is a very popular and entertaining event. David Aynsworth, the estate manager, leads the organising team, usually in the thick of it with his many skills, and is seen here relaxing with Ted Mell after a spell of steam threshing. Harry Denton of Poole-in-Wharfedale brought a small stack of oats to be threshed during the day.

After the war when the Home Guard was disbanded, the Gargrave and District Rifle Club was formed. Captain Stephen Tempest allowed them to use outbuildings on his Broughton Hall estate as a range. Here he is at the centre of the back row with Billy Fox, Tris Cuthbert, Alistair Macdonald and Ken Ellwood. Frank Lee and Wally Holgate are the only other names I can remember in this picture from around 1970.

The next village after Gargrave is Coniston Cold and the only old photograph I have is one taken in about 1910. How well the teachers and children look!

Above: Mr & Mrs Bannister of Coniston Hall were great supporters of Skipton Band and invited them on many occasions to play at various functions. Here Mrs Bannister is seen with conductor Michael Norcross, President Ken Ellwood, and two of the ladies' committee, Mrs Ellwood and Margaret Preston.

Left: The next station along the line is Bell Busk, now closed as a result of Dr Beeching's cuts. Note the elegantly dressed stationmaster. Although small, this station was very busy. Thousands of local sheep were transported to the Eden Valley in the winter to feed on turnips. We used to catch the 6 a.m. tram from Leeds to arrive at 8 a.m. and then hike up to Malham.

Another view, with a young railway man carrying lamps. Note his fine watch and chain.

Near to Gargrave at Bank Newton is a very interesting area where we see the River Aire, Leeds–Liverpool Canal and the Skipton-Carlisle railway. The railway is seen to cross over the canal, the river and the road. The canal is taken over the river by an aqueduct and then under the road. On the left a barge has just left a lock. A series of locks between Gargrave and Bank Newton take the canal over a high point from Yorkshire to Lancashire. The Pennine Way is close to here at Gargrave.

Here is Hellifield Peel, which at one time was a fortified farmhouse. This one had its roof lead stripped off and sold some years ago and is now in a very poor state.

If we had alighted from the train at Bell Busk and walked to Malham we would have crossed this bridge and perhaps walked along to Gordale Scar. Here the village is decorated for King George VI's coronation in 1937.

Joan Hassall seen here in her cottage at Malham with her OBE, which was presented to her by Her Majesty the Queen in 1988. David Chambers published a book about her lifetime of wood engraving and drawing in 1985. Her first published work was a dust jacket for *Devil's Dyke* in 1936. This was a book of poetry by her brother Christopher Hassall. Their father was John Hassall, the famous railway poster artist, whose work included 'Come to Skegness the air is so bracing' – a scene with a jolly sailor dancing along the beach. This was followed by illustrations for *Portrait of a Village* by Francis Brett Young in 1937, *Calling for a Spade* by Richard Church in 1939, *Cranford* by Mrs Gaskell in 1940, *The Brontë Story* by Margaret Lane in 1953, *Pride and Prejudice* by Jane Austen 1957, *Sense and Sensibility* in 1958, and *Emma* in 1962. Her prolific work also included bookplates, a stamp to commemorate the Silver Wedding of King George VI and Queen Elizabeth, and also the invitation cards for the coronation of Queen Elizabeth II.

This is Gordale Scar from the air. In about 1938 the City of Leeds school visited Malham; we climbed the side of the waterfall and went on up the valley to Malham Tarn. Early field systems or strip lynchets can be seen at the lower left. Watercress grows in the stream. The limestone walls are interesting, one here climbs a steep hill. They light up when the sun shines.

Following the valley up stream from Gordale we arrive at a small bridge at Mastiles Lane, a green road from Kilnsey to Malham Tarn. Walk towards Kilnsey and you will pass through a Roman marching fort for a hundred men. This appears as a large square in this aerial photograph, but is not easily discerned on the ground.

The village of Malham in 1990. There are some nice walks within Malham itself. At the top right, just short of Malham Cove, there are some very ancient walls enclosing strip fields. These date back to Anglo Saxon times. The road up past this area goes to Malham Tarn. Two roads at the lower right by Cherries Farm go to Malham Tarn and also to Gordale Scar.

The jewel in the crown of the Skipton to Carlisle railway is the Ribblehead (Batty Moss) viaduct, built between 1870 and 1874. Visit the arches and see the size of the blocks of stone – all trimmed by stonemasons on site.

Blea Moor, with its lonely signal box and water tower, is very exposed and surrounded by the Three Peaks, Ingleborough (seen here behind the box), Whernside and Pen y Ghent. After leaving Blea Moor the train plunges into the long Blea Moor tunnel and on to Dentdale.

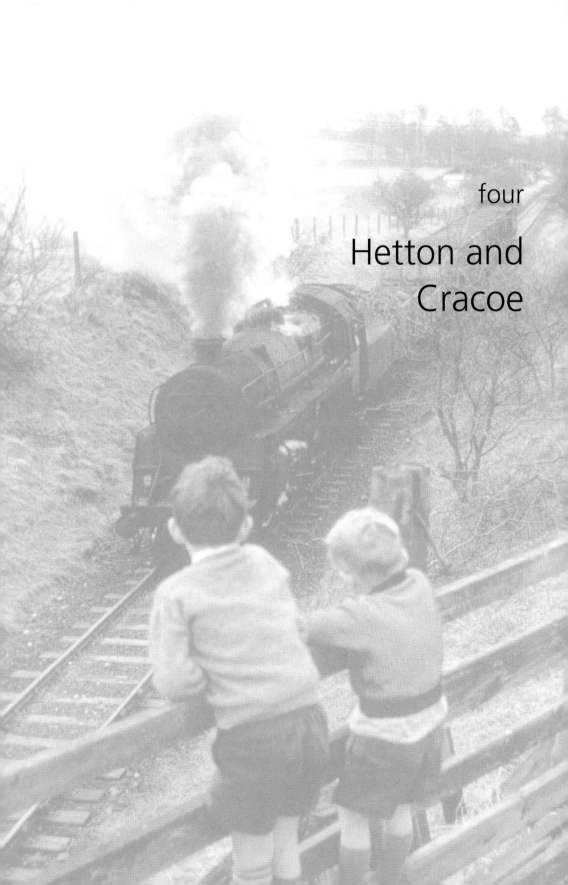

four

Hetton and
Cracoe

To the north of Skipton lies Hetton, reached by the road or by rail before 1930. Rylstone station is about half a mile away. Mr Kidd, a shoemaker of Ivy House, is on the left with Mr Child, a local policeman and part-time stonemason, who made gravestones. He lived at Wood View.

Hetton main street with a view of the Angel Inn, which now specialises in good food.

Above: Hetton from the air in August 1990. The Angel Inn, middle of picture, seems to have plenty of customers judging by the number of cars. A lovely walk can be made up Green Lane where one can enjoy the peaceful atmosphere and listen to the curlews.

Right: Two worthies of Hetton. James Reeday, a farmer, is on the left, with John Kidd, who was a shoemaker – probably more clogs than shoes.

Above: In June 1988 I was asked to photograph Rylstone and District Women's Institute and never in my wildest dreams could I have imagined what would happen to them later. When Angela Baker lost her husband John to cancer after a long illness, the women decided to do something for charity to remember him. The now world-famous nude calendar was produced by twelve of the members and raised an enormous sum of money. This has been followed by a film and a second calendar featuring the stars of the film, including Helen Mirren and Julie Walters, who plays Angela. Angela is visible in this picture standing fifth from the left, middle row.

Right: Walter Stoney with his 1928 Sunbeam model 9, which he used right through the Second World War when he was a sergeant flight mechanic with 101 Squadron. A wing commander tried many times to persuade Walter to sell it to him but eventually the wing commander went missing on ops and was never seen again. When travelling home to Hetton all the way from Norfolk in winter, Walter said he would often call in at Leeds railway station for 'a jar of tea'. Cups were in short supply.

Opposite above: Two miles to the east of Hetton is the village of Cracoe and here is an aerial view of the school, which served both villages. The school dentist is visiting, as shown by the dental caravan, which I used in my rounds as a dental surgeon, from 1954 until 1960. The Village Hall on the left was an ex-prison camp hut from Raikes Road, Skipton. This camp is featured on page 118 of my last book on Skipton.

Below: Top class at Cracoe school in 1922. At the top right is Walter Stoney, who was a very clever mechanic. Many farmers relied on his skill, especially at hay time. His skills were put to good use when he served with 101 Squadron. Amongst his memorabilia is a letter from the mother of an Australian crewmember thanking him for his conscientious work on their Lancaster bomber. His best friends are all in the top row, especially Harry Reeday (second from left). From left to right, top row: Stephen Wood, Harry Reeday, Norman Walker, Walter Stoney. Middle row: Miss D.L. Smith (headmistress), May Dugdil, Bessie Carr, Lillian Howarth, Mary Wood. Bottom row: Gwendolyn Carr, Mary Todd, Gracie Swales, Ivy Norton.

The school in 1955 or '56 with two popular teachers – Mrs Rymer on the left and head teacher Miss Kinder on the right. Whilst away in the USA on a scholarship, Miss Kinder had them all writing very newsey letters to me. I still have them. To my knowledge all have done well and there is a PhD among them!

Just past the school was the Bull's Head Inn, which was closed around 1917 and is now a private house. At an earlier date it was the New Inn.

An earlier view of the Bull's Head Inn – notice the unmade road. Near Cracoe there were roadside areas where men sat all day 'stone napping' and arranging them in neat piles. Walter Stoney told me that on their walk home from school they passed two lots of 'nappers' and on passing the second old man his pal said 'There's a chap back theer that's napped mair steans than thee'. He waited until he was fairly well past before he shouted this – the 'nappers' were good shots with a stone!

The Devonshire Inn at Cracoe – now a popular place for locals and visitors.

Above: An aerial view of Cracoe in 1990. The Devonshire Hotel is in the centre; the car park at the rear is a good landmark. In the colour original there are fields of colour, perhaps buttercups.

Left: Two popular members of the community before the Second World War were Dawes Carlisle and John Willy Hebden, who was a butcher in Cracoe.

Opposite below: Another photograph from Dawes Carlisle showing himself at Coxon's Farm in Cracoe, so called after the family that used to live there.

Above: A photograph from Dawes Carlisle showing his father, on the left, with a cross-bred dairy shorthorn at the last Skipton show, which was held in a field up the Bailey, Skipton. Mr Carlisle is presenting a trophy.

Above left: Steam trains hold a fascination for small boys. John and Peter Ellwood watch a coal train heading for Swindon Quarry in about 1967. *Above right:* An early petrol-driven drill used for making holes for blasting, *c.* 1920. It could also be used for drilling boreholes.

Opposite above: Swindon Quarry, showing the road which went through the works and also the railway passing by on the right on its way to Threshfield. It now terminates here at the quarry and the new road is roughly in the position of the railway and so bypasses the quarry works. The row of houses has been demolished. Just in view behind is a farmhouse that was an inn, called Catchall.

Opposite below: Faith, Hope and Charity Stockdale, born at Knowle Bank near Bordley in 1857.

Cynthia Rymer with Mary Stoney, who was a wonderful worker for Hetton Methodist church. Mary was the wife of Walter Stoney. see p 64, 65.

Cynthia Rymer is on the left with Helen Jackson and the Sunday school children, in around 1988.

five

Into Wharfedale

Above: The Yorkshire Dales Railway was formed in 1895 after earlier more ambitious schemes were cancelled. Even then, there was still opposition so eventually a nine-mile railway was accepted, this being from a branch near Embsay to Threshfield near Grassington. Here we see the ceremony of cutting the first sod by Walter Morrison MP of Malham Tarn House. This took place at Threshfield on 7 June 1900.

Left: This picture of the ongoing construction was taken from a glass plate loaned to me by Dr Raistrick of Linton, who wrote many books about the Yorkshire Dales. As you can see there was a lot of pick and shovel work. William Haines Hutchinson won the construction contract with a price of £29,892.

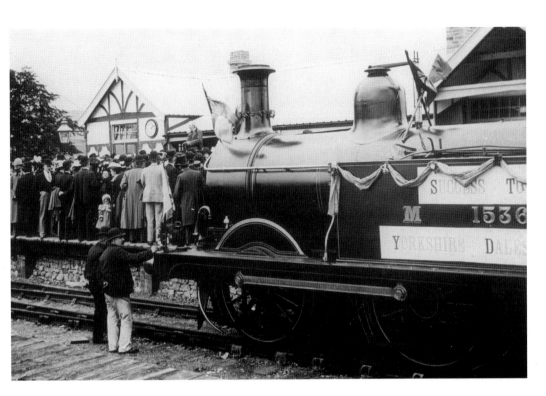

Above: This was the first train
to arrive at Grassington station,
on 29 July 1902, and there was
quite a celebration. The time
on the clock is just past 2 p.m.,
and the gentleman addressing
the crowd looks like Walter
Morrison. The engine is a
Midland Railway 0-4-4T,
No. 1536.

Right: Another photograph
from the collection of
Dr Raistrick, a rare one of a
steam shovel. The fells in the
background near Grassington
showing Grass Wood give the
rough location near to
Swindon Quarry.

The first train with passengers in ten carriages arriving at the station, hauled by another Midland Railway 0-4-4T. Passenger traffic ceased on 22 September 1930, but the line stayed in use for goods such as coal and also limestone removal from the two quarries. This still goes on today and spares the roads, which were never designed to carry heavy traffic. I have a Yorkshire Dales Railway Directors Report to Shareholders at their half yearly Ordinary General Meeting on 30 August 1909. The report gives the number of passengers booked at stations on the Midland line to Rylstone and Grassington. During first half of 1908, 23,307 were booked to Grassington, and in the second half 28,705.

Grassington is a few miles east of Cracoe and lies across the River Wharfe in a sunny position. I worked here with the dental caravan in the late 1950s and found that almost all those born and bred there were farmers and farm workers. Just a few years ago I was talking to one of them and he said ,'When you were working at the school we called it G'ston, then it became Grassington and now it's Graaasington.' Here is a Victorian picture of G'ston.

A view of the bridge over the Wharfe and the road up to the village. Strip lynchets, or medieval field systems, can be seen to the right.

Down by the river was Linton Mill, which was powered by this huge waterwheel, and here we see workmen breaking it up in April 1912. It was replaced by a steam engine, and also water turbines. When Bentley's demolished the mill to make way for houses they donated the engine to Bradford Industrial Museum, and it is now in full working order. At one time the turbines were used to generate electricity and supplied all of Grassington. It was then owned by the Lowcock family. It was a cotton mill and later rayon was used for ties, etc. It closed in 1959.

The Wilson's Arms at Threshfield was the meeting place on this occasion for the Craven Harriers. This is now a nursing home.

In 1955 two Fowler ploughing engines came by road from Wolverhampton to dredge Grimwith reservoir. Between the two of them they dragged a large scoop across the drained reservoir. The other engine stands by the wall in the distance. The cable can be seen on a drum under the boiler. Photograph by Frank Woodall.

Above: If anything interesting happens in the district, there is always an interesting man to record it. In this case it was Frank Woodall who was a Friend of the Craven Museum in Skipton. Here he is with his 1931 Morgan. He was a skilled precision engineer, who along with Griff Hollingshead repaired to working order all the antique clocks in the museum. He was soon on site at Grimwith when the engines appeared.

Right: Near to Grimwith Resevoir is Stump Cross Cavern, which is open to the public. In about 1960 I went with the Craven Pothole Club into the caverns, which were not then open to visitors. Here is Tom Pettit, head of craft and design at Aireville school, Skipton, and on the right Edgar Smith, who worked at Rolls Royce. Edgar was husband to May, who is in the Land Army photograph (see page 115).

Left: An aerial view of Grassington from a Tiger Moth G–APCU in June 1959. From the lower part of the photograph upwards we can see Celtic fields, remains from the Romano–British period (AD 200-400), Grassington village, and above are the Cracoe reef knolls including Elbolton. Grassington bridge and the River Wharfe are also in view.

Below: A friend took this photograph before I set off to photograph Grassington and Bradley, where we lived in 1959. This Tiger Moth was on of three based at the Yorkshire Aeroplane club at Geadon near Leeds. It is now in Holland.

Opposite above: In the various clearings in Grass Wood on the edge of Grassington there are many remains of early habitation. Here is a direct overhead view of a section known as Site A, thought to be Iron Age. Also to be seen at the top is a pond, and at the lower left is a line of bell pits.

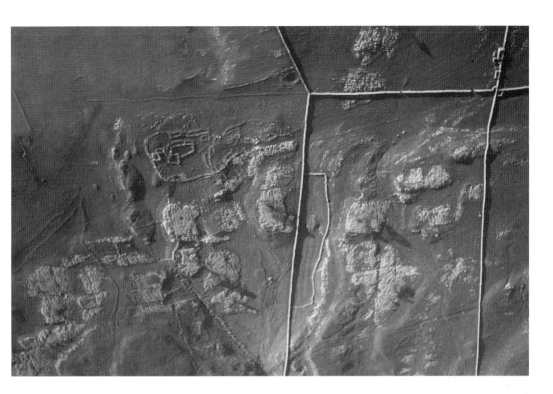

Below: The village of Conistone to the north of Grassington may be reached by a road to the east of the River Wharfe, which passes through Grass Wood. The route west of the river is via Threshfield and Kilnsey. Passing the Anglers Arms (now a private house) in 1903 is this traction engine hauling a disused railway coach. It was to become a weekend residence for someone and I think it was on the hillside near Kettlewell. There were many of these, but they had to be removed when the area became a National Park.

Left: An aerial view of Kilnsey Show, which is very popular with Dalesfolk and visitors alike. It sits snugly below Kilnsey Crag, which is used as the route of the fell race. The old hall has now been restored, and to the right is the popular café, shop and fishpond, which are run by the Roberts family.

Left: An aerial view of Conistone with St Mary's church surrounded by trees.

Opposite above: Kilnsey Show in 1953 or '54, before it became very commercial and swamped by tents. Holding their Swaledale sheep for judging are Laurie Whitehead, first on left, Jack Alderson, third, and Brian Fawcett, fifth, all farmers from Swaledale. Note the limestone walls in the background.

Opposite below An early view of Conistone village, *c.* 1900.

A 1927/28 scene outside Conistone with Kilnsey school, with head teacher Miss Ormoroyd. From left to right, back row: William Mallinson, Arnold Hall, Norman Daggett, Walter Ibbotson, Ellis Spink, Aubrey Spink, Phillip Hall. Second row: Herbert Metcalfe, Richard ?, Doris Metcalfe, Margaret Ibbotson, Margaret Daggett, Mary Robinson, Annie Ibbotson, Elsie Joy, Miss Ormoroyd. Front row: John Joy, Alfred Metcalfe, Doreen Richmond, Kathleen Hill, Rene Campbell, Hazel Ibbotson, Doris Hill, Thomas Lister.

Left: Soon after the Second World War, a Wellington bomber took off from Silverstone Operational Training Unit, and due to bad weather it crashed near Gillhouse above Conistone. A lot of the wreckage is still there. Here is an engine showing the cylinders and splined shaft.

Opposite below: A group of farm workers building a stack using pitchforks and a hay rake. The worker on top was a 'displaced person' from Europe, who settled here after the Second World War.

Above: On the road to Kettlewell east of the river there was a farm called Throstles Nest. It was farmed by Charles Horner and his sister Elsie, seen here in around 1950. The implement behind them is a hay rake.

Above: The very steep hill east out of Kettlewell on the road to Coverdale is called Park Rash and was a popular venue for motor bikers. Regular meets for this hill climb drew quite large crowds and plenty of excitement.

Left: Kettlewell from the air. The Park Rash road climbs out of the village, passes along the river valley, and climbs the steep hill at top centre to Coverdale. This is where the bikers were in the last picture. The village is now well known for its Scarecrow Show.

Opposite below: A Yorkshire Dale, Wharfedale, is the site of the only Ladies Slipper orchid that grows in Britain. Here it is in 1975.

Above: On 31 January 1942, a Wellington bomber with a Polish crew crashed on Walden Moor near Buckden Pike. The crew were on a training exercise from the operational training unit at Bramcotes in Northamptonshire. The only survivor was Joe Fuzniak, who made his way through the snow to the White Lion at Gray where he was comforted by the Parker family. Mrs Spink was only a small girl then and she said they thought he was German. They raised the alarm but the rescue party had to fight their way through snow only to find no survivors. Joe set about getting planning permission to build a memorial and one day in 1972 my son John and I went to help him. Mr Coats had given him permission to use old wall stone so we set about laying down a base. We soon realised that the rest should be done by someone with more experience in use of stone. I asked Harry Smith of Bradley to help so he soon had it ready for the stone cross. Harry carried all the cement powder up there on his back and used water from a pond. Mr Coats took the cross up on his Landrover. Here you see the finished monument with Mrs Spink, John Ellwood and Mr Coates. Joe, on the right, now lives in Bexleyheath, Kent. The small fox on the left-hand corner is in honour of the fox tracks Joe followed through the snow to safety. The story is on the internet at www.buckdenpike.co.uk.

Left: Dent Gill, a retired farmer of Hebden, lent this picture of his uncle, William Gill, who was a shoemaker at Buckden. His shop served also as the Telegraph Office and was near the Buck Inn. In the 1920s Dent was a small boy and remembered his uncle with a mouthful of nails!

Below: If we go past Kettlewell and left at Buckden along a winding road in Langstrothdale beyond Yockenthwaite, we come to Oughtershaw. In 1956 this was the furthest outpost of schools in the West Riding area, and still had no electricity. Head teacher Miss Ormeroyd had nine pupils. One boy was at home helping with sheep dipping. A dentist from Chelsea who was touring the Dales stopped by and spent the afternoon with us. He couldn't believe it! I was using a foot engine with treadle wheel. He offered me a job and if I had accepted, this epistle might never have been written.

John Hammond and his family lived at Amerdale House, now a hotel and much altered. They were wealthy landowners. I believe the house was altered in 1870.

On the west side of the valley after leaving Kilnsey there is a turnoff left and the road goes up to Arncliffe in Littondale. Here is Joe Ibbotson, a carrier who could take people to catch a train. He was also the postmaster. Jim Jowett is also pictured; he was a clog-maker.

Remember the picture on page 20 of Manby & Bro. in Skipton High Street, who also had an iron foundry? This is one of their products in the cottage of Mrs Gill in Arncliffe. She keeps this old fire range in beautiful condition. The plaque is at the top of the range.

John Hammond with his shooting party on the grouse moor, *c.* 1880. He is drawing a stick which will show him his peg number or position to stand for the drive. The shotguns are muzzle loaders.

Above: A view of Arncliffe from the hillside shows the drive to the vicarage, no longer there. The winding road up the side of the valley goes over to Darnbrook and Malham. The church and cotton mill are on the right of the picture. Cowside Beck runs down the valley into the Skirfare.

Right: Arncliffe, 16 May 1989, very much as it is today. Compare this with the photograph taken when the vicarage drive was in existence. The roads on each side of the valley and also the one climbing away up the hillside to Malham are clearly visible in this photograph.

The school dentist J.K. Ellwood and assistant Barbara Wood, with children at Arncliffe school. The head teacher was Miss Riley. The camera set on a timer and sitting on the wall has Chris Battersby wondering what will happen.

West Riding Dental Unit in the schoolyard. All these school photographs were originally in colour.

six

Burnsall and
Appletreewick

Above: Burnsall is about two miles down river from Grassington, an attractive village that lies next to a bend in the River Wharfe. This picture of the village dates from 1900. The now very mature trees along the bank of the river towards the bridge are very small with tree guards. St Wilfred's thirteenth-century church and grammar school, dated 1602, are clearly to be seen. The school has two storeys and has mullioned windows.

Left: Burnsall photographed from the south, with the lovely bends in the River Wharfe. Up river can be seen Loop Scar, thought to be part of the South Craven fault, a geological feature.

Above: Along the footpath towards the bridge one gets a good view of the Methodist chapel, built in 1901.

Right: From the air the lynchets or field systems become clearer. All the strips are a way of making level areas for crops on a hillside. This is a particularly good view of them near Thorpe, which is quite hidden away from the road on the left from Grassington to Burnsall and beyond.

Above: Next to the bridge is the village green and here we see an early car rally, probably in the early 1920s. This is not an antique car meeting, but a meeting of modern cars at that time.

Left: During periods of heavy rain up the valley the river rises rapidly and can even flood the village green. It can cover the road and touch the steps of the Wharfe View Café.

Opposite below: Wharfedale Café before it was rebuilt and named Wharfe View Café. This café is very popular with walkers and hikers on the Dales Way. It is ably run by two young farmers' wives, Heather and Jennifer, so there is plenty of home cooking. The pump is one of three compensation pumps in the village supplied by Bradford Corporation Water Works when they purchased the water rights. This picture dates from around 1950.

Above: These cottages were at one time a textile mill erected by William Tempest, taking power by means of a waterwheel powered by Joy Beck. An older mill on this site, constructed by Henry Yonge in 1672, had fallen into a dilapidated condition and so was demolished. New Mill worked as a textile mill until 1825 and was then sold by Sir Charles Tempest to Bradford Corporation Water Works for £800. They then had the water rights.

Above: A Dales bus outside the Red Lion Inn, *c.* 1930. Notice the conductor's ticket machine and leather moneybag. These buses were the lifelines of the village.

Below: An early charabanc outside the Red Lion, before the First World War.

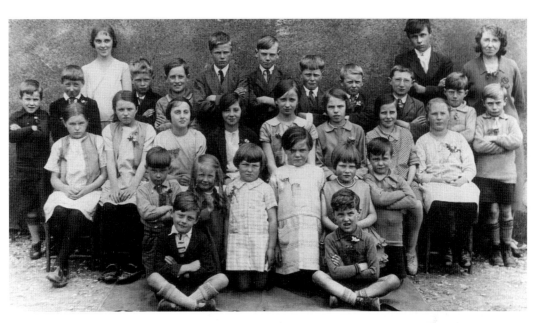

Further down the valley is another pretty village called Appletreewick. The school photograph was taken in 1929. Second from left on the back row is Irvine Newbould, who was one of the aircrew killed in the Second World War. From left to right, back row: Leonard Horton, Irvine Newbould, Muriel Sanderson (teacher), Herbert Reynoldson, Gordon Holme, George Reynoldson, Tot Reynoldson, Ted Newbould, Johnnie Payley, Frank Rodwell, David Holme, Norman Webster, Mrs Lumb. Middle row: Gladys Houseman, Rene Houseman, Margaret Hargreaves, Phyllis Lumb, Rene Newbould, Sally Wellock, Rhoda Ellison, Nora Hawley. Front row, kneeling: Hartley Spencer, Ena Horton, Marjorie Hargreaves, May Simpson, Peggy Reynoldson, Tim Horton. Sitting in front: Frank Holme, Bill Naylor. Len Horton is now president of the famous Burnsall feast and sports committee, whose annual event is held every August.

In 1987 Taylor's of Loughborough repaired the bells of St Wilfred's church. George Burfitt is positioning a bell ready to be hauled up into the tower by Mick Reid; Howard Riley is on the left. The bells were the last to be cast by Dalton of York.

Left: Appletreewick shown here in 1990 with the Craven Arms, far left, and New Inn, immediately to the left of the village.

Below: To help raise money for Skipton Brass Band, the band members performed a sponsored march through thirty villages in 1977. It was a beautiful day and a good time was had by all. Here they are marching past the New Inn at Appletreewick.

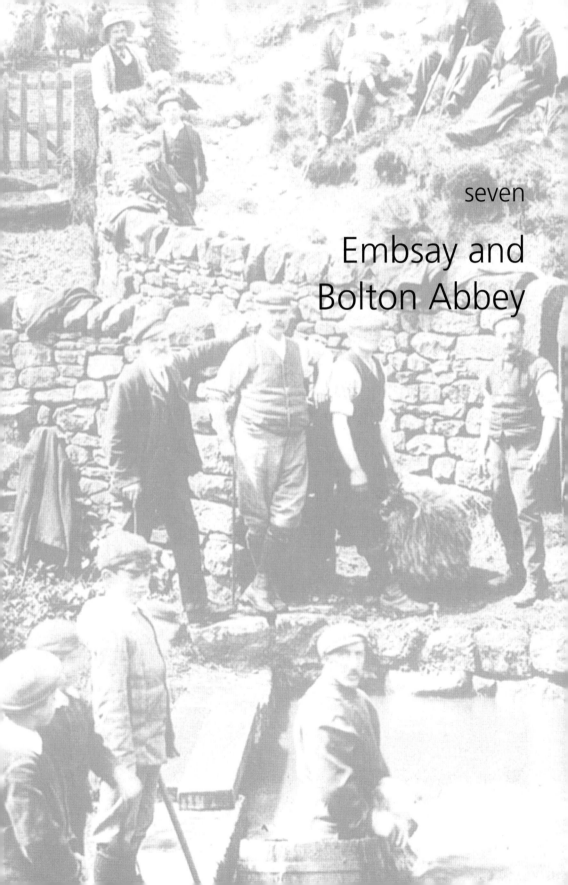

seven

Embsay and
Bolton Abbey

An early view of Embsay station and part of the village. The fields to the right of West Lane show the position of the council estate.

Left: The preserved Embsay & Bolton Abbey steam railway, Brackenley Lane, Embsay reservoir and Crookrise, seen on 28 June 1994.

Opposite below: Sheep washing on the moor above Embsay Crag. Notice one man standing in a barrel. There is also a party watching and enjoying a picnic

Above: Burrell 3918 *Deborah* at Embsay station during one of their many open days. This could be a period picture as there are no TV aerials, but in fact it was 1970.

Above: An LNER (London & North Eastern Railway) locomotive No. 3442 approaching Skipton from Ilkley. The track to the left goes up to Grassington.

Left: An almost plan view of Embsay & Bolton Abbey Steam Railway on 24 June 1994. Quite a lot has happened, such as the building of the base and track for the new shed on the left. Coaches are standing on it.

Opposite above: A clear view of Embsay British school. Does anyone know the date?

Below: When working as school dentist I met many Dales children and found them to be very friendly, so I photographed many of them. Here is Rosamund Dodd at Embsay school. Rosamund later became one of the Rylstone WI and appeared in the famous calendar as Miss November. Rosamund is also featured in the new calandar, made after the film, which includes Helen Mirren and Julie Walters. She appears in the new calendar as Miss April.

The flood at Millholme shed on 3 May 1908. The Skipton fire brigade were called in to power-wash the mud away from the looms.

This large mill was situated on the Embsay side of Eastby. If you go along there now it is hard to believe it ever existed.

In 1954 a friend alerted me to this cuckoo chick in Embsay recreation ground. It was on the ground and lucky to be alive. Kath placed it carefully back into quite a low nest in the rear hedge (a wooden fence has now replaced this).

This railway was closed down in the late 1960s by Dr Beeching, who was commissioned by the Government to make the rail system profitable, or perhaps not to lose as much. Work began immediately, but a group of enthusiasts asked William Foster, a solicitor, to obtain an injunction to halt the lifting of the lines at the station. It is a long story but the group increased in membership and, ably led by John Keavey, relaid the track and got permission to restore the station at Bolton Abbey. Sir Robert McAlpine generously rebuilt this. A copy of the station was built like the one in this photograph, which became derelict.

A local passenger train has arrived from Ilkley and will be going to Skipton via Embsay.

Class 4 MT 2642 No. 42093 local passenger train from Ilkley. Beamsley Beacon can be seen in the background.

Telegraph office and Bolton Abbey Post Office next to the Green. The building is now a bookshop.

Bolton Priory seen here from the Storiths side of the River Wharfe. A good footpath can be taken to this viewing point from Storiths about half a mile away. It is a priory and was never an abbey, and was founded in 1151 by Alicia de Romilly. Her mother had endowed a priory for Augustinian canons at Embsay in 1120. Alicia transferred them to Bolton.

Above left: Bolton Priory with the entrance not complete. Work commenced on the west tower in 1520, but was abandoned in 1539 due to the Dissolution of the Monasteries.

Above right: Bolton Priory showing the entrance tower restored and the roof complete. The work was completed in 1984. Neil Hartley was the architect.

Left: Harold Macmillan, the former Prime Minister, was often a guest of the Duke and Duchess of Devonshire to join a shooting party on the famous grouse moors. Here he is seen talking to Mr Billy Stitt, who was head keeper. Compton Wilson, whose father was head keeper years ago, is in the background. They lived in Intake and had two or three miles to walk to catch the train to Bolton Abbey to attend Ermysted's Grammar school. Eventually he and his brother Robert became boarders.

The Duke of Devonshire is leading a shooting party from High Reservoir House to Barden Beck shooting butts for the first drive of the day. Harold Macmillan is also in the picture. These pictures were loaned by Anthea Mitchell, a relative of Compton Wilson, bringing up the rear in the picture.

James Stitt was head keeper of Bolton Abbey Estate between 1932 and 1959. This is not a tame grouse, but one really defending its territory. Probably coaxed off a wall by Mr Stitt, it is ready to fly at him, and as you see Mr Stitt has gloves on and his right had ready to defend his face.

Barden Tower is described by Nikolaus Pevsner in his book *Buildings of Britain* as an impressive tower house of the time of Lord Clifford the Shepherd Lord, which is at the time of Henry VIII (1509-47). Lady Anne Clifford restored it in 1658/59. Pevsner describes the position in Wharfedale as exquisite.

Skipton Band marching past Barden Tower, a short distance up river from Bolton Priory. They were on their sponsored march through thirty villages to raise money for the band.

eight

Skipton and the
Dales at War

Left: The Land Army girls played a huge part in the war by taking over from men who were serving in the armed forces. This picture shows Dora Varley at a ploughing competition.

Below: Corn was grown in the Skipton Auction Co. fields at Carleton. Here is Dora driving a tractor, which is pulling a binder operated by Tom Glynn.

Right: Relaxing with some music from the accordion are Frances Kirkley, Dora Varley, May McCarthy (now Smith) and Dora Brownhill. May told me it was very hard work on the farms on Silsden Moor. May was the wife of Edgar Smith, a keen member of Craven Pothole Club. Many years ago he took me along passages of the Stump Cross Caverns not open to the public.

Below: Why is this photograph of Ship buildings included in the war chapter? Because it shows a sign pointing to an air-raid shelter. These signs were very common during the war.

KRIEGSGEFANGEN

IN SKIPTON

Leben und Geschichte
deutscher Kriegsgefangener
in einem englischen Lager

Herausgegeben unter Mitwirkung
vieler Kameraden von

SACHSSE und COSSMANN
Kapitän z. S.   früher Oberleutnant d. R.

MÜNCHEN 1920 / VERLAG VON ERNST REINHARDT

Above: A group of Royal Air Force prisoners in Stalag Luft III. In the middle row, fourth from left, is Stan Greaves, DFM, who flew with me when I took most of the aerial photographs used in this book. In July 1941 he lined up a very different type of aircraft, a Halifax four-engined bomber, when he and his crew were successful in hitting the battleship *Scharnhorst* lying at anchor in La Palice near Brest, France. They must have saved the lives of thousands of our merchant seamen, as the *Scharnhorst* was an Atlantic raider. Unfortunately, Stan and his crew were shot down soon after the bombs were released and they spent four years in a prison camp. They had flown all the way from Linton-on-Ouse, near York.

Left: During the First World War there was a prison camp for Germans situated at the top of Raikes Road. Two inmates, Kapitän zur See Sachsse and Oberleutnant Cossmann, published a book after the war, of which this is the title page. Two of the huts were used after the war, one going to Cracoe, next to the school and recently removed, and one to Arncliffe, later used by the gun club, which has also gone.

Right: Skipton had a prison camp in the Second World War and many of the German POWs were allowed to work and settle in the district afterwards. Hans Muller met and fell in love with Margaret Cockett and they were married on 23 December 1947. His friends helped to make him a suit. He was a wonderful man who was a patient of mine and was sadly missed by his friends when he died. Margaret now lives on the Isle of Man to be near her son and daughter-in-law Avril, who loaned this photograph.

Below: On 19 May 1944, Sergeant Patricia Parkinson of the Women's Royal Air Force married Flying Officer Ralph Goldie. She was stationed at Hawkinge in Kent, which was one of the Battle of Britain airfields, and Ralph was a Halifax pilot with Coastal Command stationed at Stornoway on the Isle of Lewis. The centre section of one of the Halifaxes which Ralph flew is now in the restored aircraft on display at the Yorkshire Air Museum at Elvington near York. Pat was lucky to survive a blast from a flying bomb attack when she and a friend were blown into a hedge and only suffered the loss of her tunic. Ralph's crew and Pat's colleagues attended the wedding. Pat now lives in Eastby.

Above left: Here is Barbara Wood, who can also be seen on page 24 of my last book about Skipton when she was a dental nurse with the West Riding County Council. During the Second World War she served with the ATS as a motor transport driver. Barbara now lives in Embsay.

Above right: Pilot Officer Alan Roger Wales was the first local airman to lose his life in the Second World War, on 22 June 1940. Roger was born in Gargrave on 23 September 1919 and was educated at Charney Hall, a prep. school at Grange, and later at Giggleswick school. After getting his 'wings' at No. 2 Flying Training school during the summer of 1939, he was posted to 235 Squadron at Bircham Newton in November, where he flew Fairey Battles and later Bristol Blenheims. He was confirmed as a Pilot Officer on 6 February 1940. At this time 235 Squadron was a fighter squadron, but was transferred to Coastal Command for fighter reconnaissance duties, which flew patrols over Holland. In a letter home in May 1940 he describes a 'scrap with three Messerschmit 109s'. His log book shows a few more entries and ceases after 30 May. He was officially confirmed as killed in action on 22 June 1940 over Amsterdam while flying Blenheim N3543. His two crew members, Sgt T.C. Jordan and Sgt W. Needham, were also killed.

Above left: Pilot Officer Peter Harfield Edmonds was born on 17 September 1920 at The Cottage, Embsay, and was the only son of Harfield Henry and Laura. He joined the RAF soon after war was declared and trained as a pilot. He was commissioned as a Pilot Officer and served with 19 Squadron at Fowlmere. On 28 August 1941 he was escorting Blenheims over Holland, when he was shot down and landed in the sea. Peter was seen to exit from his Spitfire but later his body was found washed up on the shore. He is buried in the village of Rokanje, south of Rotterdam. A Dutch book dealing with the war in the Rotterdam area mentions that Peter's body was at first not identified and his grave only had a wooden cross with the words 'English Airman'. He was later identified through articles found by the German Red Cross. After the war Peter's parents erected the lych gate at St Mary's church, Embsay, in his memory and his name can be seen engraved on an inside beam.

Above right: Sgt Waterworth lived with his parents and was a conductor for the West Yorkshire Road Car Company. By all accounts he was a popular and likeable young man who had a ready smile for everyone – hence his nickname 'Smiler'. He joined the Royal Air Force in September 1939, and while training as an air gunner he married Nellie Boothman, who lived at the Kings Head Hotel in Kettlewell. Sgt Waterworth joined a crew of five in 51 Squadron, which was equipped with Whitley twin-engined bombers, based in Dishforth. On the night of 26 January 1942 they took off to attack Emden in Germany but failed to return. All the crew except Sgt V.S. Mancini, a Canadian, were killed and are buried in Reichswald Forest British cemetery. A letter to Mrs Waterworth from the Air Ministry said they had been buried with full military honours in the Evangelical Cemetery at Meppen, north-west Germany. They must have been moved, perhaps after the war, to join other aircrews. Mrs Waterworth received a message of sympathy from the King and Queen, and then in June 1942 a letter from the Ministry of Pensions awarding her a pension of £1 0s 6d per week.

The weather could be a great problem and may have been the cause of the death of Sgt John Hammond Harker, who was the wireless operator of an aircraft which crashed near Brayspool in Cardiganshire. After completion of his training in August 1941, John, who had enlisted in August 1940, was posted to operational training units at Thornaby-on-Tees, Cleveland, and also to Silloth in Cumbria. From here he was posted to Ferry Training Unit at Honeybourne in Worcestershire, soon after October 1941. He was killed on 10 February 1942. Sgt Harker was married to Muriel and they had a baby daughter, who is now Mrs J.E. Stockdale, of Hebden. He was sub-postmaster at Grassington, a position in which he succeeded his father, the late W. Harker, who was widely known and esteemed in the Dale.

Sub-Lieutenant Michael Holdsworth was reported missing on active service on 23 February 1942. As there was no further news of him, he was presumed to have been killed in action. He was never found. Michael was twenty years old. He had lived with his parents George and Mabel Holdsworth, who were manufacturers in Halifax at Scargill House near Kettlewell. He was educated at Lockhurst Park and Harrow, and according to Miss Cutcliffe Hyne, of Kettlewell, he was a 'sensitive and good looking young man'. Michael joined the Fleet Air Arm, where the training was long and difficult, and included landing on aircraft carriers. After completing his training he was commissioned and posted to 830 Squadron, equipped with the Swordfish flare-dropping aircraft. At the time of his death they were shore-based at HMS *St Angelo* in Malta. There was no recorded attack on the night of 23/24 February and it is thought he was lost in the course of an unsuccessful search.

Michael and his brother, also killed in action, are both commemorated with stained glass windows in Kettlewell church.

Sergeant Arthur Newhouse (645144) was born at Troutbeck Farm, Linton. His parents were John William and Florence, who were farmers. Arthur attended Threshfield school and later Bradley school as his parents took the Slaters Arms Inn along with the farm which went with it. He joined the RAF early in the war and soon qualified as an air gunner. He joined a crew who were posted to 53 Squadron of Coastal Command based at North Coates in Lincolnshire. On 4 May 1942, they took off on a mission in a Lockheed Hudson AM530 and failed to return. The official records do not show the target, but all the crew are buried in East Cemetery, Amsterdam, section 85.

Flight Lieutenant William Abbotson Tetley DFC, who died on 29 May 1943 aged thirty-four, was a navigator from Grassington. He was killed during the Battle of the Ruhr (March to July 1943). After completing two operational tours with 78 and 35 Squadrons, Dishforth and Graveley respectively, he was asked to stand in as a bomb aimer for a fellow airman. However, his aircraft, Halifax HR 833, was intercepted and shot down by fighters over Antwerp on its way to the target. Only Sgt G.A. Jones, ironically performing Bill Tetley's normal role as a navigator, and P/O J.C. Goodson, flight engineer, escaped from the aircraft, which exploded. Bill and the rest of the crew were buried in the cemetery at Schoonselhop, Antwerp. In 1993 there was huge publicity surrounding the fiftieth anniversary of the Dambusters Raid and the loss of civilian and RAF lives. The photograph was taken on 29 September 1940 and his first tour was on Whitley bombers. None of these aircraft have survived. He was awarded the Distinguished Flying Cross during his second tour on Halifaxes, and the citation states that he helped to introduce this new four-engined bomber to operations and went on the first night raid to Le Havre on 10 March 1941.

Left: Peter Ingle lived on Burnside Avenue and was educated at Brougham Street school. He joined the RAF in early 1943 and trained as an airgunner, progressing from operation training unit to a heavy conversion unit at RAF Topcliffe. Here the crew would pick up a flight engineer to complete the seven members of the crew and learn to fly the four-engined Halifax bombers. At conversion unit most aircraft were already well used and Peter Ingles crew had Halifax R9420 which has already served with 76 and 38 squadrons. On July 25 1943, Peter and his crew were flying the Halifax when it span out of control and crashed one mile east of Linton Woods near Millbridge, Surrey. There were no survivors and Peter Ingle is buried in Skipton.

Above: Try to imagine the feelings of the Bracken family, especially the parents, when they lost two sons, Eddie and Billy, during 1943. Edward, born 1921, and William David, born 1925, were two of four sons and a daughter born to Miles and Lucy Bracken of 9 South View, Farnhill. After joining up, Billy served with 428, a Canadian squadron at Middleton St George (now Teeside Airport). Eddie was with 57 Squadron (nicknamed the Heinz squadron) at RAF Scampton, previously the home of the famous Dambuster squadron. Eddie was an air gunner and on the night of 29 July 1943, he and the crew took off in Lancaster ED931 for a bombing operation on Hamburg. The aircraft was attached by night fighters and crashed, although the location is not recorded. Only flying officer B.G.N. Kennedy, the navigator, survived and was taken prisoner.

Billy was a wireless operator in Halifax LK 906, which took off on 22 November for a bombing operation on Berlin. He never made it back as the plane was shot down and all the crew were killed. No crash site is recorded but the crew are all buried in Hanover Limmer British Military Cemetery. Billy's grave is plot 6, row a, grave 7.

Opposite below: John King was born on 5 December 1912 at 35 Brook Street in Skipton, the only son of William and Winifred. Educated at St Stephen's school, he went to work at Dewhursts Mill alongside his uncle in the dyehouse. In March 1940 he married Mary Donnelly and went to live at 37 Brook Street. After training as a wireless operator/air gunner, 1128416 Sergeant King joined a crew with No. 100 Squadron based near Grimsby. The photograph shows Jack on the extreme left with his crew in full flying gear, officiating at the start of War Weapons Week in Grimsby. On 2 September 1943 the crew climbed aboard Lancaster JA930 and took off for Berlin. They failed to return and only the bomb aimer, pilot officer E.C. Hammill, has a known grave. The rest of the crew are commemorated on the Air Force memorial at Runneymede.

Sydney Daggett was born on 24 April 1914 at Old North Cote, Kilnsey. His parents, Aaron and Maud Daggett, farmed there and Sydney attended Conistone school. As a farm worker, he was in a reserved occupation (exempt from military service) but his mother's retirement released him from this and he volunteered for aircrew in the RAF. Pilot Officer Daggett trained as a wireless operator and was posted to 10 Squadron at Melbourne, near York – a Halifax squadron. By this time he was married to Doris Robinson. On the night of 28/29 January 1944, his bomber was attached from underneath by a Junkers 88 while en route to Berlin. First the port wing tanks then the overload fuel tanks (carried in front of the bomb bay for a long journey) were set alight and the hydraulics were knocked out causing the aircraft to plummet and the skipper to order bale out. All the crew escaped except Sydney Daggett and Flt-Lt Kilsby, an Australian. No-one can explain why Sydney failed to get out.

Flying officer Thomas Geoffrey Dixon, 52613, was born in Malham in 1917. His parents, Clarence Evelyn and Mary, farmed Cherries Farm, which runs up to Gordale Scar, and he was educated at Ermysted's school in Skipton. Although he began his military career with the Army, being evacuated from Dunkirk in 1940, he joined the RAF in 1942. He trained as a pilot at Cranwell and flew Whitley bombers with 58 Squadron in the north of Scotland as part of Coastal Command and later Wellingtons with 547 Squadron at St Eval in Cornwall, patrolling the Bay of Biscay on anti-submarine and shipping strikes. These Wellingtons would carry torpedoes. On 23 February 1944, Flight Officer Dixon and his crew of nine took off on an anti-submarine mission which ended in the Scilly Isles. Short of fuel, they decided to land at St Mary's but due to the shortness of the runway the plane overshot and crashed. The propeller of the port inner engine broke off, tearing a hole in the side of the aircraft and severing Flight Officer Dixon's leg. He was taken to hospital but died soon after arrival. All his crew survived. His body was brought back to this area and he is buried at Cononley.

Flight Sergeant Algernon Early William Ayre was the son of the rector of Thornton in Craven. At the outbreak of was he joined the Army but transferred to the RAF and qualified as a bomb aimer. He served with 61 Squadron at Skellingthorpe near Lincoln and took part in sixteen operations but on the night of 11/12 May 1944 he was on a mission to Bourg Leopold in Belgium when his Lancaster bomber was shot down. There was only one survivor and there is no known grave for Flt Sgt Ayre.

Flying Officer John Smith's grave is in Embsay churchyard and his name is on the cenotaph. John was born at Bank Foot, Eastby, in 1923, the only son of Alan and May Smith. Not much is known of his early training in the RAF but the air historical branch of the Ministry of Defence states that on 22 May 1944, whilst flying a Spitfire from 53 Operational Training Unit at Kirton in Lindsey, Lincolnshire, he collided with a Wellington bomber and was killed. The inscription on his grave in Embsay reads: 'To live in hearts we leave behind is not to die'.

Flying Officer Frederick Ellis Spink DFC 151832 was born at Conistone in Wharfedale on 28 February 1921, the youngest son of Thomas Frederick and Elizabeth Anne. Before joining the Royal Air Force he won a county art scholarship to the Royal College of Art, which he would have taken up on his return to civilian life. Ellis trained as a navigator in Canada and was soon with 489 Squadron based at Langham in Norfolk, equipped with Beaufighter fighter bombers which were mainly used for anti-shipping or anti-submarine strikes. On 8 August 1944 he took off with his pilot Flight Lieutenant P.A. Hughes in Beaufighter NE 741. During action off the coast of Norway their aircraft was extensively damaged and out of control so they had to bale out. Flight Lieutenant Hughes, who survived the war, said that his parachute opened just above the water but Ellis was not to be seen. Peter Hughes rose to the rank of Air Commodore and now lives near Bromsgrove, Worcestershire. He sent the photograph below, taken by another Beaufighter navigator, which shows the crash of the crippled aircraft and Peter hanging from his parachute (far right). As there is no known grave, Ellis is remembered on the Runnymede Memorial and also on the family headstone in Conistone churchyard. He can be seen in a school photograph on p84.

Flight Sergeant John Grimshaw was born in Bingley, the eldest son of Frank and Lavinia Grimshaw. He volunteered for the RAF in 1943, joining 99 Squadron, equipped with Liberator bombers, as a rear gunner. He was reported missing in action on 3 December 1944 when the squadron were on operations out of Calcutta to bomb Rangoon. His aircraft collided with another plane whilst over the sea and it was thought that the pilot was dazzled by the sun. A parachute was seen but there were no survivors. John has no known grave but his name is commemorated on column 434 of the Singapore Memorial.

Harry, second left, was the son of Percy and Clara Booth who lived in School House, Draughton. He trained as a wireless operator with the RAF and was posted to 158 Squadron based at Lissett near Driffield, East Yorkshire. On the night of his death he had joined another Halifax crew to stand in for their regular wireless operator, who had been granted home leave to get married. That probably saved his life at the cost of Harry Booth's. On the night of 23 August 1943 the crew he had temporarily joined took off in Halifax HR 725 to attack Berlin. The aeroplane was shot down and while the pilot and five other crew members escaped with their lives and were taken prisoner, Harry and Sgt J.H. Jenkins, the second pilot, were killed.

Sergeant Irvine Newbould was born in Appletreewick on Christmas Day 1919. His parents were George Henry and Alice Newbould, who had Laburnum Farm but later worked the Craven Arms as a public house along with the attached farm. Many inns in those days also had farm buildings and land. Sgt Newbould was educated at Appletreewick school and left at the age of fourteen to work on the farm. Soon after the outbreak of war he joined the RAF and trained to be an air gunner. Sgt Newbould, 1495896, joined a crew at No. 70 Operational Training Unit which was based at Shandur in Egypt. Irvine lost his life when his aircraft, a Baltimore, crashed in Little Bitter Lake, one mile north of Shandur Airfield, on 12 April 1944. He is buried at Fayid War Cemetery in Egypt, plot 2, row D, grave 7. Irvine is also in the Appletreewick school photograph, p 99.